Poisonous
and Venomous Animals

THIS EDITION
Editorial Management by Oriel Square
Produced for DK by WonderLab Group LLC
Jennifer Emmett, Erica Green, Kate Hale, *Founders*

Editors Grace Hill Smith, Libby Romero, Michaela Weglinski;
Photography Editors Kelley Miller, Annette Kiesow, Nicole di Mella; **Managing Editor** Rachel Houghton;
Designers Project Design Company; **Researcher** Michelle Harris; **Copy Editor** Lori Merritt;
Indexer Connie Binder; **Proofreader** Larry Shea; **Reading Specialist** Dr. Jennifer Albro;
Curriculum Specialist Elaine Larson

Published in the United States by DK Publishing
1745 Broadway, 20th Floor, New York, NY 10019

Copyright © 2023 Dorling Kindersley Limited
DK, a Division of Penguin Random House LLC
23 24 25 26 10 9 8 7 6 5 4 3 2 1
001–333926–June/2023

A catalog record for this book
is available from the Library of Congress.
HC ISBN: 978-0-7440-7256-3
PB ISBN: 978-0-7440-7257-0

DK books are available at special discounts when purchased in bulk for sales promotions, premiums,
fundraising, or educational use. For details, contact: DK Publishing Special Markets,
1745 Broadway, 20th Floor, New York, NY 10019
SpecialSales@dk.com

Printed and bound in China

The publisher would like to thank the following for their kind permission to reproduce their images:
a=above; c=center; b=below; l=left; r=right; t=top; b/g=background

Alamy Stock Photo: Biosphoto / Daniel Heuclin 7br, 13ca, 22b, Tonia Graves 27tr, Media Drum World 17;
Dreamstime.com: Alcaproac 7clb, 17tr, Le Thuy Do 14cb, EPhotocorp 19cra, Isselee 9br, 11ca, 11cr, 11clb, Matthijs Kuijpers 6cra, 23tr,
30b, Johan Larson 24tl, Leerobin 15bl, Marco Lijoi 8t, Jason Lin 19tl, Mgkuijpers 3cb, Palex66 7cra, 18t,
Stevenrussellsmithphotos 14br, Jens Stolt 6ca, 15tr, Lukas Vejrik 7bl, 21cb; **Getty Images:** Moment / Eric Lowenbach 6clb, 26br;
Getty Images / iStock: Thierry Eidenweil 28cb, Nicoproductions 6bl, 9tl; **naturepl.com:** Daniel Heuclin 12b, 13tr,
Oceanwide / Gary Bell 7ca, 25, Constantinos Petrinos 7crb, 29tl, 29cra, Roland Seitre 21bc;
Shutterstock.com: Thorsten Spoerlein 10b, STX78 4–5b

Cover images: *Front:* **Getty Images / iStock:** Mark Kostich b; **Shutterstock.com:** n_eri;
Back: **Shutterstock.com:** Macrovector cra, Maquiladora cla

All other images © Dorling Kindersley
For more information see: www.dkimages.com

For the curious
www.dk.com

Poisonous
and Venomous Animals

Ruth A. Musgrave

DK

Contents

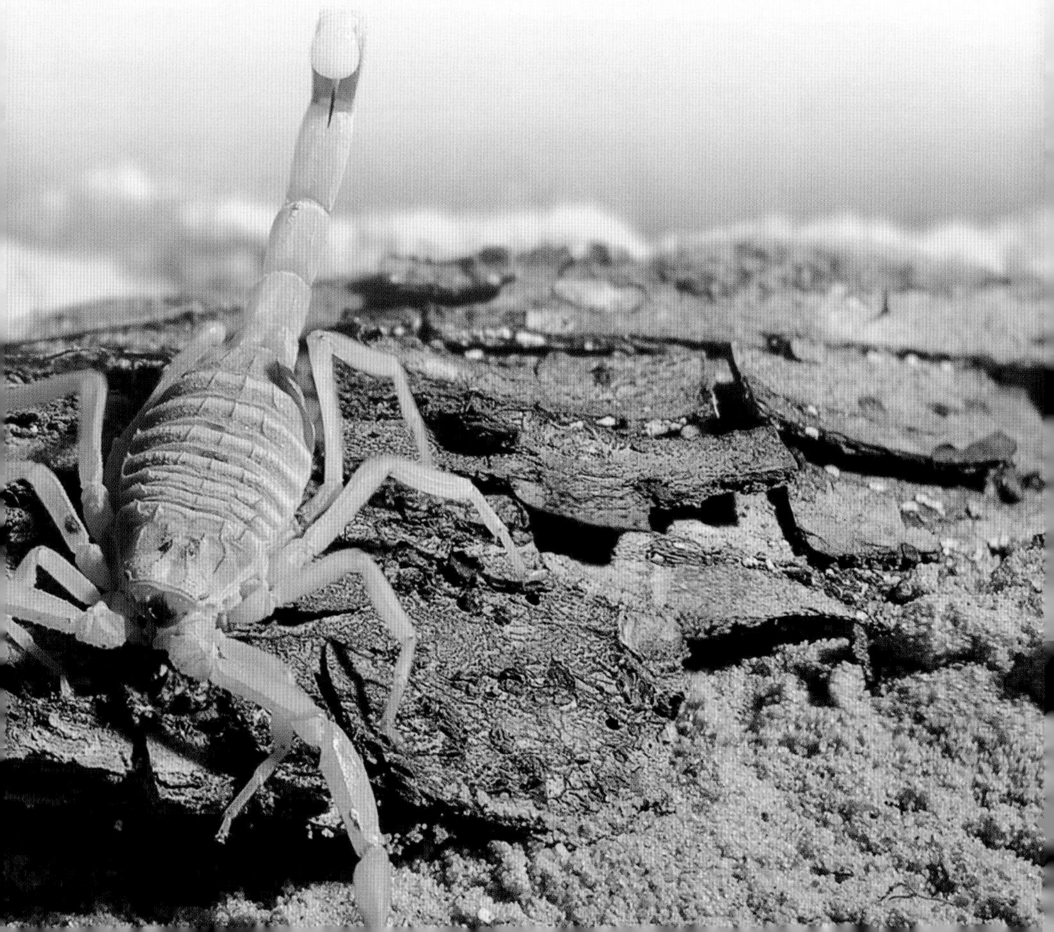

Watch Out!

Animals that are poisonous or venomous can deliver a painful, or even deadly, surprise to predators and prey.

What's the difference between poisonous and venomous? It comes down to how the animal delivers the toxin.

◆ poisonous
● venomous

Monarch Butterfly
I live in many places around the world. *(page 14)*

Black Mamba
I live in Africa. *(page 22)*

Tarantula Hawk Wasp
I live in parts of the United States. *(page 26)*

Pufferfish
I live in oceans throughout the world. *(page 8)*

Golden Poison Frog
I live in Colombia, South America. *(page 10)*

Poisonous animals often release the toxins through their skin when an animal tries to touch or eat them.

Most venomous animals share their toxins by biting, stinging, or spraying.

Let's look at—but not touch—some totally toxic creatures!

Spitting Cobra
I live in parts of Africa. (*page 16*)

Australian Box Jelly
I live in parts of the Indian and Pacific Oceans. (*page 24*)

Deathstalker Scorpion
I live in parts of Africa and Asia. (*page 18*)

Blue-ringed Octopus
I live along the coasts of Australia, Japan, and Indonesia. (*page 28*)

Duck-billed Platypus
I live in Australia. (*page 20*)

Hooded Pitohui
I live in Papua New Guinea. (*page 12*)

Pufferfish

If you see me swimming slowly through the ocean, you might think I am just another fish in the sea. But watch out.

When in defense mode, a pufferfish can inflate to several times its size! That makes it difficult for a predator to swallow. A bite of the pufferfish will deliver an unpleasant, and maybe even deadly, discovery. Pufferfish are poisonous.

Some pufferfish gulp water to inflate. Others inflate themselves with air.

A pufferfish's poison is in its skin and organs. Some predators might just get a bad taste in their mouth. Others might become numb or paralyzed. In some kinds of pufferfish, there's enough poison in just one fish to kill a predator.

Porcupinefish
The porcupinefish is a close relative of pufferfish. It has big spines that stick out.

Golden Poison Frog

It's hard not to notice me. I am only two inches (5 cm) long, but my bright yellow color almost makes me sparkle on the rainforest floor. Go ahead. Take a look. But don't touch.

This golden poison frog is the most poisonous frog on Earth. It secretes poison through its skin. Golden frogs do not make their poison. Scientists think that they get it from the tiny beetles they eat.

Golden poison tadpoles ride piggyback on their parents.

A predator that isn't warned off by the frog's bright color and tries to eat it will die quickly. One golden poison frog has enough toxins to kill 20,000 mice!

Poison Frog Species
There more than 300 kinds of poison frogs. They live in Central and South America.

Hooded Pitohui

See my bright feathers? Catch a whiff of my garbage-like smell? I'm trying to tell you something.

The hooded pitohui is a poisonous songbird that lives in rainforests on the island country of New Guinea, north of Australia.

Like golden poison frogs, this bird gets its poison from the beetles it eats. Its feathers, skin, and dander are poisonous. Most of the poison is concentrated on the bird's belly, chest, and leg feathers.

Poisonous feathers are not this bird's only defense. The hooded pitohui also has a sharp beak and claws.

When a hooded pitohui feels threatened, it raises its crest, or brightly colored head feathers. The bird's bad smell is also a warning. It tells predators, "I don't taste good!" Sneezing, burning, tingling, and watery eyes await any predator that does not heed the bird's defensive stance and stinky scent.

Predators that try to eat the bird's eggs or chicks also get an unpleasant surprise. Poison from the parents rubs off on the nest, eggs, and chicks, which protects them.

Monarch Butterfly

You can't help but notice me as I gracefully flutter through the air. But don't think my beautiful bold colors and pattern are inviting you to come closer. Quite the opposite. I'm sending a signal that says, "Stay away."

Monarch butterflies lay their eggs on milkweed, a poisonous plant. The leaves become food for the hungry caterpillars that hatch from the eggs.

Munch. Munch. The caterpillar grows bigger. It forms a pupa. About two weeks later, a butterfly unfolds from its cozy case. The toxins that the caterpillar ate remain in the butterfly.

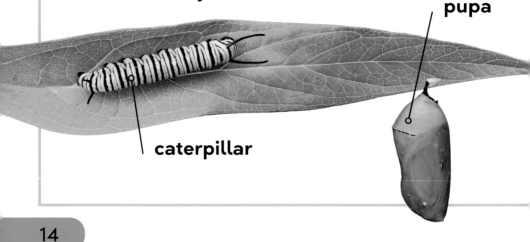

pupa

caterpillar

A monarch's coloration warns predators that it is unpleasant to eat. Scientists think that predators learn to avoid the monarch for future meals. But the monarch's method of defense isn't foolproof. Black-backed orioles, black-headed grosbeaks, and black-eared mice all eat monarch butterflies.

Viceroy Trick
A viceroy butterfly's coloration mimics a monarch butterfly's. This makes predators think the viceroy is poisonous. What a trick!

Spitting Cobra

Most venomous animals don't have bright colors to warn away predators. Their method of defense—or attack—is a bit more direct.

By the time you get this snake's warning, it's too late. When startled, spitting cobras spray venom at any animal they think is a threat.

Spitting cobras don't spit saliva. They squeeze muscles around their venom gland, which forces venom out of their fangs. They aim for the eyes. Spitting cobras have amazing accuracy and can pinpoint the eyes of an animal that's six feet (2 m) away. The venom burns, causing instant pain. This gives the cobra time to escape.

If a spitting cobra gets close enough, it will also inject venom by biting a predator or prey.

A spitting cobra's venom causes temporary or sometimes permanent damage to the eyes.

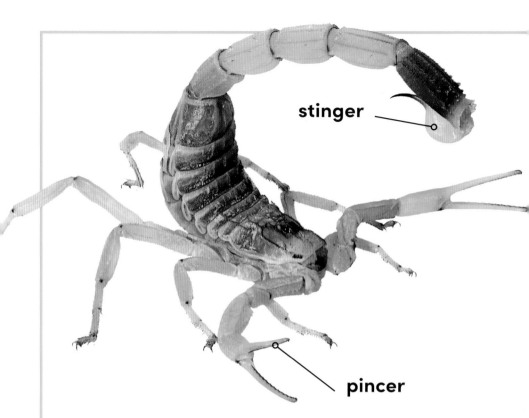

stinger

pincer

Deathstalker Scorpion

Keep your hands and feet to yourself, and I will leave you alone.

Like most scorpions, the deathstalker is a shy creature that hunts. It uses the tips of its legs to feel for prey, including spiders, grasshoppers, crickets, centipedes, and even other scorpions moving in the desert sand.

Scorpions are related to spiders. There are about 2,000 kinds of scorpions in the world.

Small but Mighty
Smaller scorpions are often more dangerous than bigger scorpions. That's because the smaller ones might depend more on their venom for survival.

When an unsuspecting insect wanders by, the scorpion rushes out and grabs the insect with its pincers. Then, the scorpion stings it with its venomous stinger.

When this scorpion needs to protect itself, it lives up to its name. The deathstalker repeatedly stabs its stinger into animals or people that bother it. The sting causes pain that can last for months. And the venom can be deadly.

Duck-billed Platypus

I keep my dangerous side hidden, unless you're another male platypus or an animal that's silly enough to grab me.

This animal is unusual. It has a bill like a duck, a tail like a beaver, and feet like an otter. Instead of giving birth to live babies like other mammals do, it lays eggs. And the male platypus is one of the world's few venomous mammals.

The platypus lives in freshwater rivers, ponds, and wetlands.

The males have a venomous spur on the back of each hind foot. During breeding season, they use their venom against other male platypuses to fight over territory and females.

The venom doesn't kill the other platypus. But the pain it inflicts might slow it down a bit, which could give the attacking platypus an advantage.

Venomous Spur
The spur of a platypus is half an inch (13 mm) long. It is connected to a gland that produces the venom.

Black Mamba

Do I have your attention? Look at my eyes. Staring straight at you. My neck flap? Flared. My mouth? Open. Hiss. Hisssss. I am angry.

The black mamba can be superfast, large, and deadly. These snakes can also be shy and secretive, but when threatened, their defenses are out in the open.

Black mambas have a flexible jaw that allows them to eat their prey, such as small mammals and birds, whole.

flared neck flap

The black mamba is named for the color inside its mouth.

The black mamba gives many warnings that it is about to strike. It hisses, spreads the hood on its neck, and opens its mouth to show off the startling black color inside. If the warnings are ignored, the snake uses its needle-sharp teeth to quickly and repeatedly bite. Each bite injects the lethal venom. Each fang has 20 drops of venom, but just two drops can kill a person if they are not treated with an antivenom.

The mamba's speed and size make it even more lethal. Black mambas are the fastest land snakes on Earth. They slither as fast as a person riding a bicycle. Large black mambas are as long as a car.

Australian Box Jelly

Now you see me... Oh wait, you don't! This venomous ocean beauty doesn't advertise or warn. In fact, the Australian box jelly's almost see-through body makes it hard to spot in the water. Victims only know they've bumped into one of these dangerous creatures when the intense, nonstop pain begins.

The Australian box jelly is one of the most venomous animals in the ocean. Its body has thousands of stinging cells. Inside each cell is a tiny, harpoon-like stinger. Touching the jelly triggers the stingers' release. Each stinger injects a fast-acting venom.

The venom causes extreme pain. If you are severely stung by a box jellyfish, you are unlikely to survive.

STINGERS

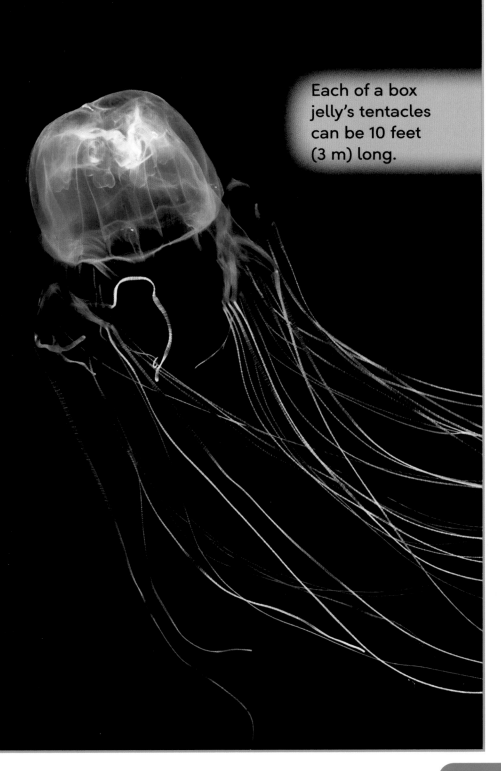

Each of a box jelly's tentacles can be 10 feet (3 m) long.

Tarantula Hawk Wasp

See my bright orange wings? They encourage you to notice my long stinger.

Tarantula hawk wasps drink nectar from flowers. Sweet, right? But female tarantula hawks have stingers that can deliver one of the most painful stings in the world.

Why does a nectar-drinking wasp need such strong venom? Females hunt venomous tarantulas. But not to eat for themselves.

Sometimes the wasp finds the tarantula out and about. Sometimes she goes right to the tarantula's burrow. A battle between spider and wasp begins. The wasp wins this time. She stings the spider, delivering the final blow.

Tarantula hawk wasps are not aggressive and will only sting if provoked.

Gentle Giants
Though big and intimidating, tarantulas are solitary and not aggressive. They do not bite or sting people unless harassed. Tarantulas use their strong jaws and venom to catch and eat prey. Or to fight the tarantula hawk wasp!

Her venom immediately paralyzes the spider but keeps it alive. The wasp drags the spider back inside its burrow. Then, she lays an egg on the spider. Before leaving, she blocks the entrance to the burrow so the egg and spider remain safely inside.

When the wasp larva hatches, it burrows into the tarantula. It eats and grows inside the still-living spider. About the time there's no spider left, the baby has become an adult wasp.

Blue-ringed Octopus

I may be little, but my flashing blue rings are a big warning. Go away.

The blue-ringed octopus is not aggressive, though it can be deadly if harassed. One species weighs less than a pencil, but its small body is filled with enough venom to fatally paralyze ten 165-pound (75-kg) animals.

This octopus lives in coral reefs, tide pools, and seagrass meadows.

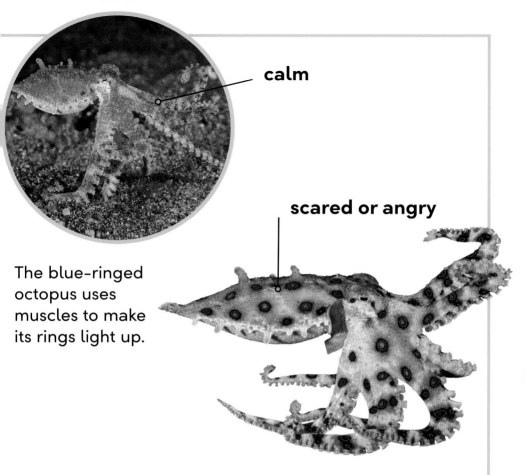

calm

scared or angry

The blue-ringed octopus uses muscles to make its rings light up.

About 25 blue rings cover its body. When the octopus is calm, the rings look faded. When scared or angry, the animal's blue iridescent rings flash like warning lights in the water. The octopus can adjust the intensity of the blue color around its rings and the speed of its flash.

When it comes to poisonous or venomous animals, beware!

Glossary

Antivenom
A medication that counteracts venom

Camouflage
An animal's coloration, pattern, or behavior that helps it hide

Dander
Dust created by flakes of an animal's skin, feathers, or hair

Paralyze
To make an animal unable to move part or all of its body

Pincers
The front claws on an insect like a scorpion

Pupa
The stage of life when a caterpillar changes into a butterfly

Stinger
The sharp barb that an animal uses to injects toxins

Toxin
A poison or venom created by a plant or animal

Index

Quiz

Answer the questions to see what you have learned. Check your answers in the key below.

1. True or False: Poisonous and venomous animals deliver their toxins in the same way.

2. What does it mean if an octopus flashes blue rings?

3. What is the most poisonous frog on Earth?

4. What kind of butterfly looks like the poisonous monarch butterfly?

5. Where are the venomous spurs on a male platypus found?

6. What animal spits through its fangs?

7. Where does the hooded pitohui get its poison from?

8. True or False: A pufferfish's poison is its only defense.

1. False 2. It is angry or scared 3. Golden poison frog 4. Viceroy butterfly 5. On the back of each hind foot 6. Spitting cobra 7. The beetles it eats 8. False